T0115527

DO NOT OPEN!
THE STORY OF PANDORA'S BOX

by Joan Holub
illustrated by Dani Jones

Ready-to-Read

Simon Spotlight

New York   London   Toronto   Sydney   New Delhi

Dear kids,

Long ago, Greeks wrote stories called myths. These stories helped them to understand things that were happening in the world around them. Myths also taught lessons about right and wrong. Some characters in mythology do things that are impossibly amazing or flat-out wrong to help teach us what *not* to do in real life!

—J. H.

SIMON SPOTLIGHT
An imprint of Simon & Schuster Children's Publishing Division
1230 Avenue of the Americas, New York, New York 10020
Text copyright © 2014 Joan Holub
Illustrations copyright © 2014 Dani Jones
All rights reserved, including the right of reproduction in whole or in part in any form.
SIMON SPOTLIGHT, READY-TO-READ, and colophon are registered trademarks of Simon & Schuster, Inc.
For information about special discounts for bulk purchases, please contact Simon & Schuster Special Sales at
1-866-506-1949 or business@simonandschuster.com.
The Simon & Schuster Speakers Bureau can bring authors to your live event. For more information or to book
an event contact the Simon & Schuster Speakers Bureau at 1-866-248-3049 or visit our website at
www.simonspeakers.com.
Manufactured in the United States of America 0522 LAK
4 6 8 10 9 7 5 3
Library of Congress Cataloging-in-Publication Data
Holub, Joan.
Do not open! : the story of Pandora's box / by Joan Holub ; illustrated by Dani Jones. — First edition.
pages cm. — (Ready-to-read)
Summary: An easy-to-read retelling of the Greek myth of Pandora, whose curiosity leads her
to open a box marked "Do Not Open!" and let loose all kinds of trouble.
1. Pandora (Greek mythology)—Juvenile fiction. [1. Pandora (Greek mythology)—Fiction. 2. Mythology,
Greek—Fiction.] I. Jones, Dani, 1983- illustrator. II. Title.
PZ7.H7427Do 2014
[E]—dc23
2013004550
ISBN 978-1-4424-8497-9 (pbk)
ISBN 978-1-4424-8498-6 (hc)
ISBN 978-1-4424-8499-3 (eBook)

Long ago
the Greeks wondered why
their gods sometimes let
bad things happen to them.
They wrote this story
to answer that question.

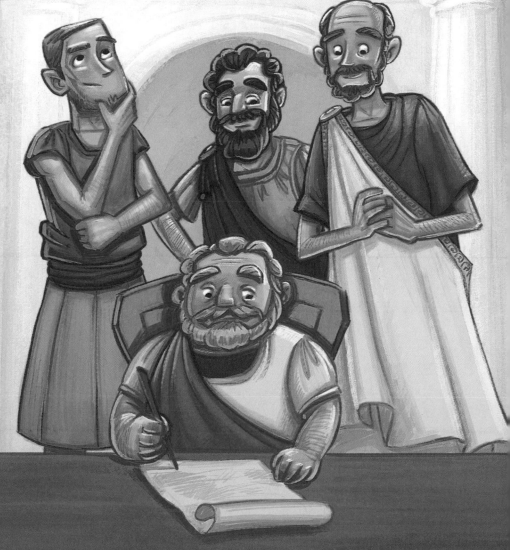

There once was
a woman named
Pandora (Pan-DOOR-uh).

She was smart and friendly.
She was also very curious.

Pandora lived with her husband,
Epimetheus (ep-eh-MEE-thee-us).
They were very happy.
So was everyone else in Greece.

The gods took care of them.
But the people were not thankful.
The gods decided
to teach them a lesson.

So the Greek gods sent a box
to Pandora's house.
It was gold and shiny.
"Who sent it?" asked Epimetheus.
"Who cares?" said Pandora.
"I love presents!"

"Let's open it," said Pandora.
"No!" said Epimetheus.
"There is a note on it.
It says: 'Do not open!'"

"Just forget about that box,"
Epimetheus warned Pandora.

But Pandora could not forget.
She wanted to know
what was inside the box.
She could not think
about anything else.

Maybe the box is full of candy,
thought Pandora.

She sniffed at the edges
of the box.
She did not smell any candy.

Maybe the box
is full of music,
thought Pandora.
She listened to the box.
But she did not
hear any music.

I will open the box,
Pandora decided.
I will look inside.
Then I will close it again.
Epimetheus will never know.

*Maybe the box
is full of jewels,*
thought Pandora.
It could make us rich!
She tried to peek.
But she could not see inside.

Pandora pulled on the box's lid.
It did not open.
She pulled harder.
And harder.

Suddenly the box popped open.
Hundreds of bugs flew out!
They stung Pandora.
"Ow! Ow!" she yelled.
Just then Epimetheus ran in.
The bugs stung him, too.

"Why are you hurting us?"
Epimetheus asked.
"Because we are trouble bugs!"
they said.

The trouble bugs flew outside.
They made trouble
everywhere they went.
People began to fight.
They got sick.
They felt sad.
Even the flowers drooped.

"Look what you have done!"
said Epimetheus.
"I am sorry," said Pandora.
She shut the box.
But it was too late.
The world was already full
of trouble.

"Let me out!"
shouted a tiny voice.
"Who said that?"
asked Epimetheus.

"It came from the box,"
said Pandora.
"There is something else
inside of it."
Pandora opened the box again.

A fairy flew out.

"Who are you?" asked Pandora.

"I am Hope," said the fairy.

"I help people in trouble."

Hope kissed Pandora's
bug bites.
She kissed Epimetheus's
bug bites.
Right away they felt much better!

"Now I must say good-bye,"
said Hope.
"I must go help other people, too."

"Wait!" cried Pandora. "What if we need you again?"

"I will always come back when you need me," promised Hope.

The fairy flew away.
Soon she brought hope
to everyone in the world.

And she kept her promise
to Pandora and Epimetheus.
Hope always returned
when they needed her.

Sometimes bad things happen.
But we hope things will get better.
And we hope
for good things to happen.

What do you hope for?

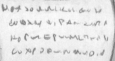